MASTERING BUSINESS

PLANNING IN 2024: A

Comprehensive Guide

Traci Fischer

Table of contents

Introduction

In the ever-evolving world of entrepreneurship, success is reserved for those who dare to dream, but even more so for those who possess the unwavering determination to turn their dreams into reality. If you find yourself on the precipice of launching a new venture or steering your existing business to new heights in 2024, you've embarked on a journey filled with both exhilarating possibilities and formidable challenges.

The keys to unlocking these possibilities and overcoming those challenges lie within the pages of this comprehensive guide. "Mastering

Business Planning in 2024" is not just another manual but a tailored compass that will help you navigate the dynamic and unpredictable business landscape of tomorrow.

In an era marked by unprecedented innovation, ever-changing consumer behavior, and global connectivity, the rules of business are continually being rewritten. The strategies that led to success yesterday may not suffice tomorrow. This book is your bridge to the business world of 2024, a world where adaptability, foresight, and strategic acumen are the currencies of achievement.

Why, you may ask, is a business plan so vital in this rapidly changing landscape? The answer lies in the essence of planning itself. As Benjamin Franklin wisely said, "By failing to prepare, you are preparing to fail." In the same vein, crafting a solid business plan is your preparation for the unpredictable journey ahead. It's your blueprint, your compass, and your strategic roadmap.

Our aim is to equip you with the knowledge, insights, and tools to craft a business plan that is not just a static document but a living, breathing framework capable of guiding your business through the turbulent tides of 2024 and beyond.

In these pages, we'll explore the nuances of defining your business vision, conducting market research, creating a winning business model, building a robust operational plan, and formulating innovative marketing and sales strategies in an era dominated by digital disruption. We'll delve into the intricacies of financial projections and risk mitigation, ensuring your business remains robust even in the face of uncertainty. We'll guide you on how to attract funding and investments, and provide you with real-world case studies that exemplify the art of exceptional planning.

As we venture through this journey together, we'll also explore the role of technology in modern business planning and discover how it can streamline your efforts, facilitate collaboration, and enhance the efficiency of your strategic pursuits.

Beyond the business plan, we'll unravel the secrets of sustainable growth and long-term success, ensuring your business remains relevant, resilient, and ready to thrive in an era where the only constant is change.

So, whether you're a budding entrepreneur poised to launch your first startup or a seasoned business owner aiming to revitalize your strategy, this guide is your faithful companion. It's designed to empower you with the insights and tools you need to navigate the complexities of business in 2024, chart a course to success, and adapt to the ever-shifting tides of opportunity.

The world of business is a vast, challenging, and ever-transforming realm, but with the right plan and a dedicated spirit, you can navigate it with confidence and seize the boundless opportunities it offers. "Mastering Business Planning in 2024" is your guide, your confidant, and your ally on this thrilling journey into the future of commerce.

So, let's embark together, for the future of your business begins right here, right now. The world of 2024 awaits, and we're ready to help you conquer it.

Chapter 1

Defining Your Business Vision - Setting the Course for Success

In the grand tapestry of business, every successful venture begins with a singular thread – a compelling vision. Your business vision is more than just a distant dream; it is the North Star that guides your decisions, fuels your passion, and propels your enterprise forward. In this first chapter of "Mastering Business Planning in 2024," we will explore the significance of a clear and inspiring vision and how to define one that resonates with the essence of your enterprise.

The Power of a Vision

"Where there is no vision, there is no hope." - George Washington Carver

At the heart of every great enterprise lies a vision, a statement of purpose that defines why the business exists and the impact it aims to create. Your vision is your rallying cry, your source of motivation, and your ultimate destination. Without it, a business can drift aimlessly, and its prospects of long-term success can become uncertain.

But what sets an exceptional vision apart from a mere slogan? It's the power to evoke emotion and inspiration. A compelling vision serves as a unifying force, attracting talent, investors, and customers who share your enthusiasm for the future you imagine. It is a potent tool for creating a brand identity that resonates with your target audience.

In 2024, this principle holds truer than ever before. With a global business landscape characterized by fierce competition, rapid technological advancements, and a conscientious consumer base, having a well-crafted and authentic vision can mean the difference between thriving and fading into obscurity.

Defining Your Vision

1. Look Inward:A strong vision often starts by looking within. Reflect on your own passions and values. What motivated you to start this venture in the first place? What kind of impact do you want to have on the world, your industry, or your community?

2.Think Long-Term:Your vision should transcend short-term goals. Think about where you see your business in five, ten, or even twenty years. What legacy do you want to leave behind?

3. Consider Your Audience: Understand your target audience's needs and aspirations. A vision that aligns with your customers' desires is more likely to create a loyal following.

4. Be Authentic: Authenticity is key. A vision that genuinely reflects your values and intentions will resonate more with stakeholders. Avoid empty, clichéd statements.

5. Inspire and Motivate: Your vision should inspire both your team and your customers. It should be a source of motivation that keeps everyone focused on a common goal.

Crafting Your Vision Statement

The culmination of your contemplation and soul-searching is your vision statement – a concise, memorable declaration of your business's purpose and aspirations. While there is no one-size-fits-all formula for creating a vision statement, there are key elements that can guide your journey:

1. Clarity: Ensure your vision is clear and easy to understand. Avoid jargon or overly complex language. Make it accessible to all stakeholders.

2. Conciseness: Keep it succinct. A great vision can be encapsulated in just a sentence or two. It should be easy to recall and share.

3. Inspiration:Your vision should inspire. It should evoke emotions and aspirations. Reading it should make your team and customers feel excited about the future.

4. Alignment: Your vision must align with your mission and values. It should serve as a bridge between where you are now and where you want to go.

5. Future-Oriented: A vision should be future-oriented, focusing on what you aim to achieve in the long term.

Let's explore some real-world examples of compelling vision statements that have resonated with customers and driven businesses to remarkable success:

- Tesla: "To create the most compelling car company of the 21st century by driving the world's transition to electric vehicles."

- Google:"To provide access to the world's information in one click."

- Disney:"To make people happy."

- SpaceX:"To enable humans to become a multiplanetary species.

- Airbnb: "To create a world where anyone can belong anywhere."

In each of these cases, the vision statement is clear, inspirational, and future-oriented. It encapsulates the essence of the respective businesses and has been a driving force in their achievements.

In the ever-evolving business landscape of 2024, your vision will be your anchor in times of uncertainty, your guiding light in the darkest of storms, and your beacon of hope for your team and customers alike. It's more than just words on paper; it's the foundation upon which you will build your business empire.

Closing Thoughts

As we venture further into the intricate world of business planning, always remember that your vision is not a static statement. It is a living entity that should evolve as your business grows and adapts to changing circumstances.

Chapter 2

Market Research and Analysis - Navigating the Shifting Tides of 2024

In the dynamic landscape of business, knowledge is power. The second chapter of "Mastering Business Planning in 2024" propels us into the realm of market research and analysis, where we'll uncover the tools and strategies to understand the intricate currents of the marketplace. In a world marked by rapid change and relentless innovation, staying afloat requires more than just a business plan; it demands a deep, data-driven understanding of your market.

The Essence of Market Research

Imagine setting sail on a voyage across the vast ocean of business without a map or a compass. You wouldn't do it, would you? Yet, many entrepreneurs venture into the world of commerce without the necessary navigational tools. Market research is your map, your compass, and your telescope, allowing you to chart a course, stay on track, and foresee the challenges and opportunities that lie ahead.

Market research is the systematic process of gathering, analyzing, and interpreting data about a market, including its size, growth potential, consumer preferences, and the competition. It is the foundation upon which every successful business plan is built. In 2024, where market dynamics are evolving at an unprecedented pace, robust market research is the lifeblood of smart decision-making

The Key Components of Market Research

1. Understanding Market Trends: Keeping a finger on the pulse of your industry is essential. What are the latest trends, emerging technologies, and shifts in consumer behavior?

By identifying and adapting to these trends, you can position your business ahead of the curve.

2. Analyzing Consumer Behavior: In an age when data is abundant, understanding your target audience has never been more critical. What do consumers desire? How do they make purchasing decisions? By comprehending their behavior, you can tailor your products and marketing efforts effectively.

3. Competitive Analysis: The competitive landscape is ever-evolving. Who are your competitors? What are their strengths and weaknesses?

Conduct a thorough competitive analysis to identify opportunities to differentiate your business.

4. SWOT Analysis: A SWOT analysis helps you evaluate your business's internal strengths and weaknesses, as well as external opportunities and threats. It's a valuable tool for strategic planning.

Navigating Market Research in 2024

Market research in 2024 is a multifaceted endeavor, reflecting the rapid pace of change in business and technology. Here's how you can navigate this shifting landscape effectively:

1. Embrace Data-Driven Decision Making:In the digital age, data is the linchpin of market research. Leverage big data analytics, customer relationship management (CRM) tools, and artificial intelligence (AI) to gain actionable insights into your market.

2. Monitor Real-Time Data:The business landscape is no longer static. Real-time data monitoring is essential for staying ahead. Use tools to track social media trends, website analytics, and consumer sentiment.

3.Tap into Predictive Analytics: Predictive analytics can help forecast market trends and customer behavior. These tools use historical data to make educated predictions about future market dynamics.

4. Conduct Surveys and Focus Groups: Direct feedback from your target audience is invaluable. Utilize online surveys, focus groups, and feedback forms to understand your customers' needs and expectations.

5. Explore Global Markets: In a world interconnected as never before, consider the potential of expanding into global markets.

International market research opens up new horizons for growth and innovation.

Real-World Examples

Let's examine how some prominent companies have harnessed the power of market research to their advantage:

- Netflix: The streaming giant became a powerhouse through its data-driven approach. By analyzing user behavior and preferences, Netflix tailors its content recommendations, which keeps viewers engaged and subscribed.

- Amazon: Amazon's mastery of data analytics allows it to optimize pricing, recommend products, and even forecast inventory needs. The result is an exceptional customer experience and a dominant market position.

- Apple: Apple's success can be attributed to in-depth market research. It pays meticulous attention to customer feedback, leading to the creation of products that resonate with user needs and desires.

- Spotify: The music streaming service uses data to recommend personalized playlists and songs, making it a go-to platform for music enthusiasts.

These companies didn't merely stumble upon their success; they meticulously researched their markets, harnessed the power of data, and adapted to ever-changing consumer preferences.

Closing Thoughts

In the evolving business landscape of 2024, market research isn't an optional step; it's a strategic imperative. Without a clear understanding of the market you operate in, your business plan risks being adrift in a sea of uncertainty.

Chapter 3

Crafting a Winning Business Model - The Blueprint for Success in 2024

In the ever-evolving landscape of business, a winning business model is akin to a ship's sturdy hull. It provides the structure and direction your business needs to navigate the often turbulent waters of commerce. In the third chapter of "Mastering Business Planning in 2024," we embark on a voyage to explore the nuances of crafting a business model that's not just resilient but primed for success in a world defined by rapid change, innovation, and shifting consumer preferences.

The Role of Your Business Model

A business model is the framework that outlines how your enterprise operates, generates revenue, and creates value for its customers. It's the master plan, the architectural design, and the engine of your business all rolled into one. In 2024, a business model is more than just a strategy; it's a dynamic blueprint that adapts to the ever-changing marketplace.

Your business model encompasses key elements:

1.Value Proposition: What unique value does your business offer to customers?

2. Revenue Model: How will your business make money? What is your pricing strategy?

3. Market Segment: Who are your target customers, and what are their characteristics?

4.Channel: How do you reach your customers? What distribution channels do you use?

5. Customer Relationship: How do you build and maintain relationships with your customers?

6. Key Resources and Activities: What are the critical assets and operations required to deliver your value proposition?

7.Partnerships: Are there strategic alliances or partnerships that bolster your business?

8. Cost Structure: What are the key costs associated with running your business?

The Business Model Canvas

One effective tool for visualizing and developing your business model is the Business Model Canvas. This one-page framework provides a clear and concise way to dissect and build your business model. It consists of nine building blocks, as illustrated below:

1.Customer Segments: Who are your customers, and what are their specific needs?

2.Value Proposition:What products or services solve the customer's problems or fulfill their needs?

3.Channels: How do you reach your customers, and how do they prefer to be reached?

4. Customer Relationships: What type of relationships do you establish with your customers (personal, automated, etc.)?

5. Revenue Streams:How do you generate revenue from your value proposition (sales, subscriptions, licensing, etc.)?

6.Key Resources: What assets and resources are vital for delivering your value proposition?

7. Key Activities: What crucial tasks or activities are required to make the business model work?

8. Key Partnerships:Are there external organizations or entities that are essential for your business's success?

9. Cost Structure: What are the major costs associated with your business operations?

Using the Business Model Canvas can help you map out your current business model and identify areas for improvement or innovation. It's a versatile tool that fosters clarity, alignment, and a deeper understanding of how all the pieces of your business fit together.

Adapting to the 2024 Landscape

In 2024, the business environment is characterized by rapid technological advancements, shifting consumer behavior, and global interconnectedness. These factors demand adaptability and innovation in your business model. Here are some strategies to ensure your business model remains relevant in this evolving landscape:

1. Embrace Technological Disruption: Keep pace with technological advancements and leverage them to enhance your value proposition. Explore how technologies like AI, blockchain, and the Internet of Things (IoT) can improve your offerings and operations.

2. Customer-Centricity: In an era of consumer empowerment, place your customers at the center of your business model. Continuously gather feedback and adjust your model to better meet their evolving needs and preferences.

3. Sustainability and Social Responsibility: Consider how your business model aligns with sustainability and social responsibility. A growing number of consumers in 2024 are conscious of the environmental and ethical aspects of their purchases.

4. Global Expansion: Expanding into global markets can be a viable growth strategy. Assess how your business model adapts to international markets and regulatory environments.

5. Collaboration: Explore partnerships and collaborations with other businesses to enhance your value proposition and reach new customer segments.

6. Data-Driven Decision Making: In the data-rich landscape of 2024, use analytics and insights to make informed decisions about your business model. Data can reveal customer preferences, market trends, and operational efficiencies.

7. Financial Flexibility: Maintain a flexible cost structure that can adjust to changing economic conditions. Be prepared to pivot or make cost-saving adjustments when necessary.

Real-World Business Models

To better understand the concept of a business model, let's examine a few real-world examples of businesses that have successfully carved their niche by innovating their models:

1. Uber: Uber's ride-sharing platform revolutionized the transportation industry by connecting drivers and passengers through a mobile app. Their business model is built on the sharing economy, which leverages underutilized resources, such as private vehicles.

2. Airbnb: Airbnb disrupted the hospitality industry by enabling individuals to rent out their homes or rooms to travelers. Their business model is based on peer-to-peer accommodations.

3. Amazon Web Services (AWS): AWS offers cloud computing and storage services, providing

businesses with scalable and cost-effective infrastructure. Their business model is centered around pay-as-you-go cloud services.

4. Netflix: Netflix transformed the entertainment industry by offering on-demand streaming of movies and TV shows. Their business model relies on subscription-based content delivery.

5. Tesla: Tesla's business model focuses on electric vehicles, renewable energy, and energy storage. Their innovative approach combines various elements to create a sustainable ecosystem.

Each of these companies identified an opportunity to innovate the traditional business model within their respective industries, ultimately leading to their success.

Closing Thoughts

In the ever-changing world of business, your business model is the backbone of your success. In 2024, it's not enough to follow a generic template; you must adapt and innovate continually. The key is to remain vigilant, adaptable, and customer-centric.

Chapter 4

Operational Plan - Building the Engine of Your Business in 2024

In the realm of business, strategy is like the blueprint for a magnificent skyscraper, and the operational plan is the construction process that brings it to life. The fourth chapter of "Mastering Business Planning in 2024" delves into the critical role of the operational plan, guiding you through the process of building the engine that powers your business in a world defined by rapid technological advancements, global connectivity, and evolving customer expectations.

The Essence of an Operational Plan

An operational plan is the granular roadmap that details how your business will achieve its strategic objectives. It encompasses the day-to-day activities, processes, resources, and milestones required to turn your vision into a functioning business. While the business model sets the stage, the operational plan orchestrates the performance.

An effective operational plan:

- Ensures Efficiency: It streamlines operations and allocates resources efficiently.

- Guides Decision-Making: It provides a clear path for decision-making, ensuring alignment with the overall business strategy.

- Facilitates Accountability:It assigns responsibilities and timelines, promoting accountability within the organization.

- Measures Progress: It establishes key performance indicators (KPIs) to measure success and identify areas for improvement.

- Adapts to Change: It allows for flexibility and adaptability in the face of unexpected challenges or opportunities.

In 2024, the operational plan is more than a document; it's a dynamic and responsive framework that drives your business forward, enabling it to thrive in a world of constant change.

The Components of an Operational Plan

An operational plan comprises several key components, each serving a distinct purpose in guiding your business:

1. Business Processes: Detail the operational processes that your business will follow, from product development to order fulfillment and customer service.

2. Resource Allocation: Specify how resources, including financial, human, and technological, will be distributed to support your operations.

3. Roles and Responsibilities: Clearly define the roles and responsibilities of each team member within your organization.

4. Timelines and Milestones: Create a timeline that highlights key milestones and deadlines necessary for the successful execution of your operational plan.

5. Key Performance Indicators (KPIs): Identify the KPIs that will be used to measure the success of your operations. This could include metrics related to sales, customer satisfaction, production efficiency, and more.

6. Risk Management: Outline potential risks and challenges that may arise during your operations and develop strategies for mitigating or addressing them.

7. Technology Integration: Explain how technology will be integrated into your operations, including software, hardware, and other digital tools to enhance efficiency and productivity.

8. Scalability and Growth: Consider how your operational plan supports business scalability and growth. How can your operations expand to meet increased demand or adapt to market changes?

Crafting Your Operational Plan

Developing an operational plan involves a comprehensive process. Here's a step-by-step guide to creating a compelling and effective plan:

1. Define Your Objectives: Start by clearly defining your operational objectives. What are

you trying to achieve through your day-to-day activities and processes?

2. Analyze Your Current State: Assess your existing operations to understand what is working well and where there is room for improvement. Identify bottlenecks and areas that need optimization.

3. Allocate Resources:Determine the resources required to execute your operational plan, including finances, staff, technology, and physical assets.

4. Design Processes:Detail the operational processes that will be in place, from product

development to customer service. Document these processes for clarity and consistency.

5. Assign Roles and Responsibilities: Clearly define the roles and responsibilities of each team member within your organization. Ensure that each person understands their specific duties.

6. Set Timelines and Milestones: Develop a timeline that outlines key milestones and deadlines. This helps create a sense of urgency and accountability.

7. Establish KPIs: Identify the key performance indicators that you will use to measure the success of your operations. These should align with your objectives.

8. Address Risks and Contingencies:Identify potential risks that could disrupt your operations and develop strategies to mitigate these risks.

9. Integrate Technology: Determine how technology will be integrated into your operations, including software, hardware, and other digital tools to enhance efficiency and productivity.

10. Plan for Scalability and Growth: Ensure your operational plan is flexible and capable of adapting to changes in demand and market conditions. Consider the long-term scalability and growth potential.

Adapting to the 2024 Landscape

In 2024, the operational plan is not merely about optimizing current processes; it's about staying ahead of trends and innovation. Consider these strategies to ensure your operational plan is adaptable and responsive to the evolving landscape:

1. Digital Transformation:Embrace digital tools and technologies that enhance efficiency and productivity, from AI and automation to data analytics.

2. Remote and Hybrid Work Models: If relevant to your business, explore remote and hybrid work models, allowing your team to work from

different locations while maintaining productivity.

3. Sustainability and Eco-Friendly Practices: Integrate sustainable and eco-friendly practices into your operations, aligning with consumer preferences for environmentally responsible businesses.

4. Supply Chain Resilience: Build a resilient supply chain that can adapt to global disruptions, such as pandemics or natural disasters.

5. Customer-Centric Approach:Put the customer at the center of your operational plan, focusing on personalized experiences, rapid response times, and customer feedback.

6. Regulatory Compliance: Stay updated on changing regulations and ensure your operational plan aligns with legal requirements, especially in industries subject to frequent changes.

7. Scenario Planning:Develop contingency plans for different scenarios, allowing your business to adapt quickly to unexpected changes.

Real-World Examples

Let's examine how some businesses have innovated their operational plans to thrive in the modern landscape:

1. Zappos: The online shoe retailer is known for its customer-centric operational plan. Zappos goes beyond selling shoes, emphasizing exceptional customer service and free shipping, resulting in a loyal customer base.

2. Amazon: Amazon's operational plan includes innovations like robotic fulfillment centers, Prime delivery services, and machine learning algorithms that anticipate customer preferences.

3. Netflix: Netflix's operational plan emphasizes personalized content recommendations powered by algorithms and user data, creating a highly engaging and sticky service.

4.Airbnb:Airbnb's operational plan leverages technology to streamline the booking process and provides a platform for hosts and guests to connect.

5. Tesla: Tesla's operational plan includes a commitment to sustainability, integrating electric vehicle production with solar energy and energy storage solutions.

These companies have redefined their operational plans to align with changing consumer behaviors, emerging technologies, and market dynamics, ultimately positioning themselves for success.

Closing Thoughts

In the dynamic landscape of 2024, a well-crafted operational plan is your North Star, guiding your business through uncharted waters. It's the bridge between your business model and your day-to-day reality, ensuring that your strategies are executed efficiently, responsibly, and with a keen eye on the future.

Chapter 5

Marketing and Sales Strategies in the Digital Age - Conquering 2024's Consumer Landscape

In the dynamic and ever-evolving world of business, your marketing and sales strategies are the sail and rudder that steer your ship toward success. The fifth chapter of "Mastering Business Planning in 2024" is a deep dive into the art and science of marketing and sales in a landscape dominated by digital disruption, shifting consumer preferences, and a global marketplace. As we explore this chapter, you'll discover how to craft strategies that attract, engage, and convert customers in 2024 and beyond.

The Crucial Intersection of Marketing and Sales

In 2024, the boundary between marketing and sales continues to blur, creating an integrated approach that serves as the foundation of your business's growth. Effective marketing serves as the initial attraction, drawing potential customers into your orbit. Sales, on the other hand, closes the deal, turning those prospects into paying customers.

A powerful synergy exists between marketing and sales, each informing and enhancing the other. In this chapter, we will examine how to orchestrate this synergy, ensuring that your marketing and sales strategies are not only aligned but also designed to thrive in the digital age.

The Digital Transformation of Marketing and Sales

The landscape of marketing and sales has undergone a radical transformation in the digital age. Traditional methods like billboards and cold calls have given way to online advertising, social media engagement, email marketing, and sophisticated analytics. This transformation has created both new opportunities and challenges, as businesses must adapt to engage with today's tech-savvy, digitally connected consumers.

To excel in the digital age, consider these key elements:

1.Data-Driven Decision-Making: Leverage the wealth of data available to make informed marketing and sales decisions. Analyze customer behavior, preferences, and engagement metrics to fine-tune your strategies.

2.Personalization:Consumersexpect tailored experiences. Implement personalization in marketing and sales efforts to deliver relevant content and recommendations.

3.Omnichannel Marketing:Reach customers across multiple channels – online, mobile, social media, email, and more. An omnichannel approach ensures consistency and maximizes reach.

4. Content Marketing:Content remains king. High-quality, relevant content is essential for engaging and educating your target audience.

5.Marketing Automation:Use automation tools to streamline repetitive marketing tasks, freeing up time for more strategic efforts.

6. SEO and SEM:Optimize your online presence through search engine optimization (SEO) and search engine marketing (SEM) to enhance visibility and attract organic and paid traffic.

7. E-commerce Integration:If applicable, integrate e-commerce capabilities into your website to facilitate online sales, offering a seamless shopping experience.

8. Social Media Engagement:Actively engage with your audience on social media platforms,

using them not only for promotion but also for building relationships and trust.

9. Customer Relationship Management (CRM): Implement a robust CRM system to manage customer data, streamline sales processes, and improve customer service.

10. Mobile Optimization: With the increasing use of mobile devices, optimize your online presence and marketing materials for mobile users.

Crafting Your Marketing and Sales Strategies
Effective marketing and sales strategies are dynamic and tailored to your unique business

and target audience. Here's a structured approach to crafting strategies that resonate with consumers in 2024:

1. Customer Persona Development:Create detailed customer personas that represent your ideal customers. Understand their needs, preferences, and pain points.

2. Content Strategy:Develop a content strategy that aligns with customer personas. Plan and create content that educates, entertains, or solves problems for your target audience.

3. Social Media Strategy:Define your social media approach. Determine which platforms

your audience frequents and establish a content calendar for consistent engagement.

4. Email Marketing Strategy: Implement an email marketing strategy that includes lead nurturing, personalized content, and segmentation for different customer segments.

5. Search Engine Optimization (SEO): Optimize your online content and website for search engines to improve your visibility and organic traffic.

6. Paid Advertising Strategy: If your budget allows, consider paid advertising on platforms

like Google Ads or social media ads. Create ad campaigns that target your ideal customers.

7. Sales Funnel Design: Map out your sales funnel, which includes the stages a prospect goes through before making a purchase. Develop content and strategies for each stage.

8. Lead Generation Plan: Develop a plan for generating leads through various channels, such as your website, social media, and email marketing.

9. Sales Team Training: If you have a sales team, ensure they are well-trained and equipped with

the tools and resources they need to close deals effectively.

10. Analytics and Reporting:Implement an analytics and reporting system to measure the success of your marketing and sales efforts. Adjust your strategies based on data-driven insights.

Adapting to the 2024 Landscape

In 2024, the digital marketing and sales landscape is marked by rapid technological advancements, evolving consumer behaviors, and global connectivity. To stay ahead, consider these strategies to ensure your marketing and sales strategies remain adaptable and relevant:

1. AI and Machine Learning: Leverage artificial intelligence and machine learning to automate tasks, personalize content, and predict consumer behavior.

2. Voice Search Optimization: With the growth of voice-activated devices, optimize your online content for voice search to stay accessible to a wider audience.

3.Social Commerce:Explore the integration of e-commerce directly into social media platforms to capture impulse buyers.

4. Video Marketing:Video content continues to dominate. Incorporate video into your marketing strategy, utilizing live streams, product demonstrations, and storytelling.

5. Chatbots and Virtual Assistants: Use chatbots and virtual assistants for real-time customer service and support, enhancing the user experience.

6. Influencer Marketing: Collaborate with influencers in your industry to extend your reach and credibility among specific target audiences.

7. Privacy Compliance: Stay up to date with privacy regulations like GDPR and CCPA to

ensure compliance in your marketing and sales practices.

8.Sustainability and Social Responsibility: Highlight your business's commitment to sustainability and social responsibility, aligning with the growing conscientious consumer base.

9. Competitive Analysis: Continuously analyze your competitors and adapt your marketing and sales strategies to differentiate yourself and offer a unique value proposition.

Real-World Examples

Let's explore how some well-known brands have effectively adapted their marketing and sales strategies in the digital age:

1. Nike: Nike's "Just Do It" campaign and strong social media presence have helped the brand maintain a strong connection with consumers. They also leverage e-commerce to drive online sales.

2. Apple: Apple's product launches, along with its minimalistic and captivating marketing, have consistently generated high demand and created a loyal customer base.

3. HubSpot:As a marketing and sales software provider, HubSpot practices what it preaches. Their content marketing strategies, including blog articles, ebooks, and webinars, attract businesses looking to enhance their own marketing and sales efforts.

4. Amazon:Amazon's mastery of data analytics and personalization results in a seamless shopping experience and cross-selling opportunities. Their marketing strategies are designed to keep customers engaged and returning for more.

5. Airbnb:Airbnb's referral program, user-generated content, and personalized travel

recommendations help keep users engaged and attract new guests and hosts.

These companies demonstrate how an effective combination of marketing and sales strategies can create a compelling and successful brand.

Closing Thoughts

In the ever-evolving landscape of 2024, marketing and sales strategies have become the fulcrum upon which business success pivots. An integrated approach that understands and engages the digital consumer is the key to thriving in this dynamic environment.

Chapter 6

Customer Experience and Retention - Building Lasting Relationships in the Digital Era

In the fast-paced world of modern business, customer experience and retention are the twin engines that drive success. The sixth chapter of "Mastering Business Planning in 2024" delves into the art of creating exceptional customer experiences and strategies for retaining those customers in an environment defined by digital disruption, abundant choices, and evolving consumer expectations. As we explore this chapter, you'll uncover the secrets to building lasting relationships with your customers, turning them into loyal advocates for your brand.

The Significance of Customer Experience

Customer experience (CX) is more than just a buzzword; it's the foundation upon which successful businesses are built. In 2024, consumers expect not only great products or services but also a seamless, personalized, and memorable experience. A positive CX can differentiate your business from competitors and keep customers coming back for more.

Here's why customer experience matters:

- Loyalty:Exceptional CX creates loyal customers who are more likely to choose your brand over others.

- Referrals: Satisfied customers become advocates, referring friends and family to your business.

- Higher Spending:Customers who have a positive experience are willing to spend more on your products or services.

- Reduced Churn:A great experience reduces customer churn, increasing retention rates.

- Brand Reputation: CX affects your brand's reputation, and positive reviews can boost your online presence.

To excel in 2024, businesses must prioritize CX, treating every interaction as an opportunity to delight, engage, and retain customers.

The Customer Journey

Understanding the customer journey is crucial in crafting a remarkable experience. The customer journey maps the series of interactions a customer has with your brand, from the initial awareness stage to post-purchase interactions. It consists of several key stages:

1. Awareness: This is where customers first become aware of your brand, product, or service.

2. Consideration: At this stage, they're evaluating their options, considering whether your offering meets their needs.

3. Purchase: The customer decides to buy from you, making the transaction.

4. Post-Purchase: After the purchase, the customer interacts with your product, service, or support. This stage is critical for retention.

5. Advocacy: Loyal customers become advocates, referring others to your business.

Mapping the customer journey helps you understand where and how to improve the customer experience. It enables you to be proactive in meeting customer needs and addressing concerns.

Strategies for Exceptional Customer Experience

To create exceptional CX in 2024, you need a well-rounded strategy that covers various touchpoints. Here are essential components of a winning CX strategy:

1. Personalization:Tailor your interactions to each customer. Use data to understand preferences and create personalized experiences.

2. Omnichannel Support:Be available on various channels – from chat, email, and social media to phone support and in-person interactions.

3. Speed and Convenience: Ensure that every interaction is efficient and convenient for the customer. Quick response times and easy processes are key.

4. Consistency:Maintain consistency across all interactions. Ensure a consistent brand voice, messaging, and quality in every touchpoint.

5. Employee Training:Equip your employees with the skills and knowledge to provide excellent customer service.

6. Proactive Support: Anticipate customer needs and address them before customers have to ask.

7. Feedback Mechanisms:Provide ways for customers to share feedback, and act on that feedback to improve your processes and services.

8. Reward Loyalty: Implement loyalty programs and rewards for returning customers.

9. Emotional Connection: Create an emotional connection with your customers. Brands that resonate emotionally tend to have more loyal customers.

10. Data Analytics: Use data analytics to gain insights into customer behavior, preferences, and

pain points. This data can inform your CX strategy.

Customer Retention Strategies

Customer retention is as important as acquisition. Retained customers spend more, refer others, and contribute to the long-term health of your business. Here are some strategies for customer retention:

1. Loyalty Programs: Implement a loyalty program that rewards customers for repeat purchases.

2. Customer Feedback:Act on customer feedback to continuously improve your products or services.

3. Personalization:Continue to personalize your communications and offerings to cater to individual customer preferences.

4.Exclusive Content:Offer exclusive content, deals, or access to loyal customers as a token of appreciation.

5.Engagement Campaigns:Create campaigns that engage existing customers through surveys, special promotions, and events.

6. Exceptional Post-Purchase Support:The post-purchase experience is crucial. Provide

excellent support and assistance during and after the customer's use of your product or service.

7. Subscription Models:If applicable, offer subscription-based services to create recurring revenue streams.

8.Customer Communication: Keep customers informed about updates, improvements, and relevant news about your brand.

9. Social Proof: Highlight customer reviews and testimonials to build trust and reassure potential buyers.

10. Exceed Expectations: Continually aim to exceed customer expectations, turning them into delighted and loyal advocates.

Adapting to the 2024 Landscape

In the digital era of 2024, customers are more empowered than ever. They have access to vast information, numerous choices, and platforms for expressing their opinions. To adapt to this landscape, consider these strategies:

1.Artificial Intelligence (AI) and Automation:Use AI and automation to personalize recommendations and interactions, streamline support, and analyze customer data.

2. Chatbots and Virtual Assistants: Implement chatbots and virtual assistants to provide real-time support and assistance.

3. Enhanced Self-Service: Provide robust self-service options, allowing customers to solve problems and find information on their own.

4. Data Security:Invest in robust data security to protect customer information and build trust.

5. Responsiveness: Respond promptly to customer queries and feedback, demonstrating your commitment to their satisfaction.

6. Social Listening: Monitor social media and online channels for customer feedback and engage in conversations about your brand.

7. Sustainability and Social Responsibility: Embrace sustainability and social responsibility

initiatives, aligning with the values of conscientious customers.

8. Community Building:Create a community around your brand where customers can connect, share experiences, and offer support to one another.

Real-World Examples

Let's examine how some notable brands have excelled in customer experience and retention:

1. Apple: Apple's excellent customer service, product quality, and brand loyalty programs have created a strong customer retention strategy.

2. Amazon: Amazon's Prime membership program fosters customer loyalty by offering benefits like free shipping, streaming services, and exclusive deals.

3. Starbucks: Starbucks has built a strong community around its brand, providing a sense of belonging and customer engagement beyond just coffee.

4. Zappos: Known for its outstanding customer service and returns policy, Zappos creates a unique experience that encourages customer retention.

5.Tesla:Tesla's commitment to sustainability and cutting-edge technology resonates with a loyal customer base, resulting in high customer retention rates.

These brands have demonstrated how a relentless focus on customer experience and retention can lead to long-lasting customer relationships and business success.

Closing Thoughts

In the fast-paced world of 2024, customer experience and retention are not just buzzwords; they are the lifeblood of a thriving business. With customers more empowered and informed than ever, creating exceptional experiences and retaining their loyalty is essential for success.

Chapter 7

Innovation and Adaptation - Thriving Amidst Change in 2024

In the fast-paced world of business, innovation and adaptation are the twin pillars upon which success is built. The seventh chapter of "Mastering Business Planning in 2024" delves into the art of innovation and strategies for adaptation in a landscape defined by technological disruption, evolving consumer needs, and global market dynamics. As we explore this chapter, you'll uncover the secrets to staying ahead of the curve, delighting your customers, and attracting buyers in 2024 and beyond.

The Imperative of Innovation

Innovation is not merely a buzzword; it's the life force that propels businesses forward. In 2024, innovation is not an option but a necessity. Rapid technological advancements, changing market landscapes, and ever-evolving customer expectations demand a mindset of continuous innovation.

Here's why innovation is crucial:

- Competitive Advantage:Innovative products, services, and strategies differentiate your business in a crowded marketplace.

- Sustainability:Innovating to enhance efficiency and reduce waste is essential for long-term sustainability.

- Growth:Innovative approaches open up new opportunities and markets for expansion.

- Resilience:Being adaptable and innovative enables businesses to withstand disruptions and unexpected challenges.

To excel in 2024, businesses must foster a culture of innovation and stay committed to finding new and better ways to meet customer needs.

The Spectrum of Innovation

Innovation is not a one-size-fits-all concept. It spans a spectrum from incremental improvements to disruptive breakthroughs. Understanding this spectrum is essential for tailoring your innovation strategies to the unique needs and goals of your business. Here's an overview:

1. Incremental Innovation:This involves making small, gradual improvements to existing products, services, or processes. It's about

optimizing what you already have. While seemingly minor, these changes can yield significant results over time.

2. Product Innovation: This is the creation of entirely new products or significant improvements to existing ones. Product innovation can open up new markets and revenue streams.

3. Process Innovation: Process innovation focuses on improving how things are done within your organization. It can lead to increased efficiency, cost savings, and better resource management.

4. Business Model Innovation:This is about rethinking the fundamental ways your business creates, delivers, and captures value. Business model innovation can lead to entirely new revenue streams or customer segments.

5. Service Innovation:Service innovation involves creating new or improved services to better meet customer needs. It often complements product innovation and can enhance customer experiences.

6. Disruptive Innovation:This is the most radical form of innovation. It involves creating new products, services, or technologies that disrupt and transform entire industries. Disruptive

innovation often requires a high degree of risk-taking.

Strategies for Fostering Innovation

Fostering a culture of innovation is not about waiting for a eureka moment but creating an environment where innovation can thrive. Here are strategies to cultivate innovation in your business:

1. Leadership Support: Innovation starts at the top. Leaders must encourage and support innovation initiatives.

2. Cross-Functional Collaboration: Encourage employees from different departments to collaborate, bringing diverse perspectives to problem-solving.

3. Idea Generation Platforms: Create platforms for employees to submit, discuss, and refine ideas. This can be through digital tools, brainstorming sessions, or innovation challenges.

4. Data-Driven Insights: Use data to gain insights into customer behavior, market trends, and areas in need of improvement.

5. Customer Feedback:Act on customer feedback and involve customers in the co-creation of products and services.

6. Prototyping:Develop prototypes or minimum viable products to test new ideas and gather feedback before full-scale implementation.

7. Risk Tolerance: Encourage calculated risk-taking. Innovations often involve some degree of uncertainty and risk.

8. Continuous Learning: Invest in employee training and development to keep skills and knowledge up to date.

9. Patience and Persistence: Recognize that not all innovations will succeed immediately. Persistence is key to refining and adapting ideas.

10. Open to Failure: Understand that not all innovation attempts will succeed, and failure is part of the innovation process. Learn from failures and apply those lessons to future efforts.

Adapting to the 2024 Landscape

In 2024, the pace of change is faster than ever. To thrive, businesses must not only innovate but also adapt to evolving market dynamics. Consider these strategies to ensure your business is agile and responsive:

1. Digital Transformation: Embrace digital technologies to enhance your operations, reach, and customer experiences.

2. Market Research: Continuously gather market data to stay informed about changing customer preferences, emerging trends, and evolving competition.

3. Agility and Flexibility: Structure your organization to be nimble and adaptable, capable of quickly responding to changes and opportunities.

4. Talent Development: Invest in the development of your workforce, ensuring they have the skills and knowledge needed to navigate evolving industry landscapes.

5. Sustainability and ESG Initiatives: Consider sustainability and environmental, social, and governance (ESG) initiatives to align with changing consumer values and regulatory requirements.

6. Scenario Planning:Develop contingency plans for various scenarios to be prepared for unexpected changes.

7. Mergers and Acquisitions: Explore opportunities for mergers or acquisitions that can expand your capabilities and reach.

8. Market Expansion: Consider entering new markets, both domestically and internationally, to diversify your customer base.

9. Regulatory Compliance: Stay informed about changing regulations and ensure your business is compliant with relevant laws.

Real-World Examples

Let's look at some companies that have excelled in innovation and adaptation:

1. Apple: Apple consistently introduces innovative products like the iPhone and iPad, revolutionizing markets and consumer expectations.

2. Tesla: Tesla has disrupted the automotive industry by pioneering electric vehicles and autonomous driving technology.

3. Netflix: Netflix has transformed the entertainment industry by pioneering streaming services and creating original content.4. Amazon: Amazon has adapted and diversified

from an online bookseller to a global e-commerce and cloud computing giant.

5. Airbnb: Airbnb innovated by connecting travelers with unique lodging experiences around the world, disrupting traditional hospitality.

These companies demonstrate how a relentless focus on innovation and adaptation can lead to transformative success and enduring relevance in the market.

Closing Thoughts

In the dynamic landscape of 2024, innovation and adaptation are the keys to not just survival but thriving in the face of rapid change. By fostering a culture of innovation, staying agile, and adapting to evolving market dynamics, your business can remain at the forefront of its industry.

Chapter 8

Marketing in the Digital Age - Strategies to Attract and Engage Buyers in 2024

Welcome to Chapter 8 of "Mastering Business Planning in 2024." In this chapter, we'll dive deep into the world of marketing in the digital age. The landscape of marketing has evolved significantly, driven by rapid technological advancements, shifting consumer behavior, and the increasing importance of online and mobile platforms. As we explore this chapter, you'll gain insights into the strategies and tactics required to attract, engage, and convert buyers in 2024 and beyond.

The Digital Marketing Revolution

In 2024, marketing is not just about advertising your products or services; it's about creating meaningful connections with your audience. The digital marketing revolution has shifted the focus from brands talking at consumers to brands engaging in conversations with them. The power now lies with the consumer, who can research, compare, and make informed decisions like never before.

Here's why understanding digital marketing is crucial:

- Visibility and Reach:Digital platforms offer a global stage, allowing businesses to reach a vast audience.

- Customer Engagement:Digital marketing facilitates two-way communication, enabling brands to engage with their customers.

- Data-Driven Decision-Making:The digital realm provides a wealth of data that businesses can use to optimize their strategies.

- Cost-Effective:Digital marketing can be more cost-effective than traditional methods, offering a high return on investment.

- Adaptability:Digital marketing allows for real-time adjustments and quick responses to market changes.

The Digital Marketing Landscape

The digital marketing landscape is vast and dynamic. To master it, you need to understand its key components:

1. Search Engine Optimization (SEO):SEO involves optimizing your online content to improve its visibility on search engine results

pages. SEO is crucial for attracting organic, non-paid traffic to your website.

2. Content Marketing: Content marketing is about creating and distributing valuable, relevant content to attract and engage a defined target audience. This content can take various forms, including blog posts, videos, ebooks, and more.

3. Social Media Marketing:Social media platforms provide an excellent channel for engaging with your audience. Each platform has its unique features and audience, making it essential to tailor your strategy for each.

4. Email Marketing: Email marketing remains a powerful tool for communicating with your

audience, nurturing leads, and driving conversions.

5. Paid Advertising (PPC): Pay-per-click (PPC) advertising allows you to display ads on various platforms and pay only when a user clicks on your ad.

6. Influencer Marketing: Collaborating with influencers in your industry can extend your reach and build credibility among specific target audiences.

7. Affiliate Marketing: Affiliate marketing involves partnering with other businesses or individuals who promote your products or services in exchange for a commission on sales.

8. Video Marketing:Video content continues to dominate, with live streams, product demonstrations, and storytelling all contributing to the video marketing landscape.

9. Mobile Marketing:As mobile device usage continues to grow, optimizing your online presence and marketing materials for mobile users is essential.

10. Chatbots and Automation:Chatbots and marketing automation tools are valuable for personalizing customer interactions and streamlining marketing processes.

Crafting Your Digital Marketing Strategy

A successful digital marketing strategy is not one-size-fits-all. It requires careful planning and customization to your specific business and audience. Here's a structured approach to crafting your digital marketing strategy:

1. Define Your Target Audience: Start by clearly defining your target audience. Who are they? What are their preferences, pain points, and behaviors?

2. Set Clear Objectives: Determine your marketing objectives. Are you looking to

increase brand awareness, generate leads, drive sales, or something else?

3. Choose the Right Platforms: Select the digital platforms and channels that align with your target audience and marketing objectives.

4. Develop a Content Strategy: Create a content strategy that includes the creation and distribution of valuable content that resonates with your audience.

5. Optimize for SEO:Implement SEO techniques to ensure your content ranks well in search engine results.

6. Plan Your Social Media Presence:Develop a social media strategy that outlines the platforms

you'll use, content calendar, and posting schedule.

7. Email Marketing Plan:If applicable, plan your email marketing strategy, including lead nurturing and personalized content.

8. Paid Advertising Campaigns: Set up and manage paid advertising campaigns, focusing on relevant keywords, ad copy, and targeting options.

9. Analytics and Measurement:Implement an analytics and reporting system to measure the success of your marketing efforts and make data-driven adjustments.

10. Customer Engagement and Retention: Keep customers engaged through post-purchase communication, loyalty programs, and ongoing relationship-building.

Adapting to the 2024 Landscape

Digital marketing is a field that constantly evolves, driven by emerging technologies and shifting consumer behavior. To stay ahead in 2024, consider these strategies:

1. Voice Search Optimization: With the growth of voice-activated devices, optimize your online content for voice search to remain accessible to a wider audience.

2. Artificial Intelligence (AI):Leverage AI for personalization, automation, and data analysis to improve customer experiences and target your marketing efforts more effectively.

3. Augmented Reality (AR) and Virtual Reality (VR): Explore how AR and VR can enhance customer engagement and experiences, especially in industries like retail and entertainment.

4. Privacy and Data Security: Maintain robust data security to protect customer information and build trust, especially in light of increasing privacy regulations.

5.Social Responsibility and Sustainability: Highlight your business's commitment to social responsibility and sustainability, aligning with the values of conscientious consumers.

6. Visual Search and Image Recognition:As visual search becomes more prevalent, consider how your products or services can be optimized for this technology.

7. User-Generated Content:Encourage users to create and share content related to your brand, which can enhance authenticity and engagement.

8. Community Building:Create a community around your brand where customers can connect,

share experiences, and offer support to one another.

9. Niche Marketing: Focus on niche marketing to reach specific, highly targeted audiences.

Real-World Examples

Let's examine how some well-known brands have excelled in digital marketing:

1. Nike: Nike has leveraged influencer marketing, content creation, and social media engagement to maintain a strong digital presence.

2. Coca-Cola: Coca-Cola consistently launches creative and engaging marketing campaigns

across various digital platforms, often incorporating user-generated content.

3. Airbnb: Airbnb uses a blend of user-generated content, video marketing, and social media campaigns to create a compelling online presence.

4. Red Bull: Red Bull is renowned for its content marketing, focusing on extreme sports and unique experiences, which resonates with its target audience.

5. HubSpot: HubSpot itself excels in digital marketing, providing a wealth of content and tools that help businesses optimize their digital strategies.

These brands have demonstrated the power of digital marketing to engage and attract buyers, build strong online communities, and remain relevant in a rapidly changing landscape.

Closing Thoughts

In the digital age of 2024, mastering the art of digital marketing is essential for attracting, engaging, and converting buyers. The strategies and tactics discussed in this chapter are your roadmap to navigating the complex and dynamic

digital marketing landscape.

Chapter 9

Sales Strategies in the Modern Marketplace - Converting Leads into Loyal Customers in 2024

Welcome to Chapter 9 of "Mastering Business Planning in 2024." In this chapter, we will explore the intricacies of sales strategies in the modern marketplace. Sales have transformed significantly in the digital age, and mastering these strategies is vital for converting leads into loyal customers in 2024 and beyond.

The Shifting Landscape of Sales

The modern sales landscape is marked by significant changes. Traditional sales methods have given way to more customer-centric and data-driven approaches. As a result, customers are more empowered, informed, and demanding than ever before.

Here's why understanding modern sales strategies is crucial:

- Customer-Centric Approach: Modern sales focus on the needs and preferences of customers, creating a more personalized and engaging experience.

- Data-Driven Decisions:Data and analytics play a central role in understanding customer behavior and improving sales strategies.

- Omnichannel Sales:Customers can interact with businesses through various channels, and sales strategies must adapt to this multichannel environment.

- Empowered Consumers: Consumers have access to a wealth of information and choices, making it essential for businesses to provide value and build trust.

The Sales Funnel in the Digital Age

The traditional sales funnel has evolved in the digital age. It now encompasses a series of stages that a prospect goes through before making a purchase. Understanding these stages and adapting your sales strategies to them is vital. The typical stages include:

1. Awareness: At this stage, a prospect becomes aware of your brand, product, or service, often through marketing efforts.

2. Interest: The prospect starts showing interest and begins to research and consider your offering.

3. Consideration: During this stage, the prospect evaluates your product or service, compares it with alternatives, and weighs the benefits.

4. Intent: The prospect intends to make a purchase but may still have questions or concerns.

5. Evaluation: This stage involves evaluating specific product options, pricing, and other details.

6. Purchase: The prospect decides to make the purchase.

7. Post-Purchase: After the purchase, the customer interacts with your product or service,

receiving support, using the product, and forming an impression.

8. Loyalty and Advocacy: Loyal customers become advocates and may refer others to your business.

Strategies for Effective Sales

To master sales in the modern marketplace, you need a well-rounded strategy that covers various aspects of the customer journey. Here are key components of a successful sales strategy:

1. Customer Persona Development:Create detailed customer personas to understand their needs, preferences, and pain points.

2. Sales Team Training: Ensure your sales team is well-trained, equipped with the tools and resources they need to effectively engage with prospects and close deals.

3. Sales Funnel Design: Map out your sales funnel, detailing the specific strategies, content, and interactions for each stage.

4. Lead Generation Plan:Develop a plan for generating leads through various channels, such as your website, social media, and email marketing.

5. Content Strategy: Develop a content strategy that aligns with customer personas and the sales

funnel, creating content that educates and nurtures leads.

6. Sales Enablement Tools: Provide your sales team with tools and technology that enhance their productivity and effectiveness, such as customer relationship management (CRM) systems.

7. CRM Implementation:Implement a robust CRM system to manage customer data, streamline sales processes, and improve customer service.

8. Analytics and Reporting: Implement an analytics and reporting system to measure the

success of your sales efforts, allowing you to make data-driven adjustments.

9. Lead Scoring: Use lead scoring to prioritize and focus on leads that are more likely to convert into customers.

10. Sales Follow-Up: Develop a structured follow-up process to ensure no potential leads slip through the cracks.

Adapting to the 2024 Landscape

Sales strategies must evolve with the changing marketplace. To succeed in 2024 and beyond, consider these strategies for adapting to the evolving landscape:

1. Artificial Intelligence (AI): Leverage AI for predictive lead scoring, chatbots for customer support, and data analysis to better understand customer behavior.

2. Automation: Implement automation tools to streamline routine tasks, freeing up time for your sales team to focus on more strategic efforts.

3. Sales Tech Stack: Invest in a tech stack that includes CRM, marketing automation, and sales analytics tools to enhance your sales efforts.

4.Personalization: Use data to personalize interactions and tailor your sales messages to each prospect.

5. Mobile Optimization: Ensure that your sales materials and processes are optimized for mobile users, as the use of mobile devices continues to grow.

6. Omnichannel Sales: Meet customers on the channels they prefer, whether it's email, social media, or in-person interactions.

7. Social Selling: Actively engage with your audience on social media platforms, building relationships and trust with potential customers.

8. E-commerce Integration: If applicable, integrate e-commerce capabilities into your website to facilitate online sales, offering a seamless shopping experience.

9. Video Sales Calls: Incorporate video calls into your sales process, offering a more personal touch in a remote working environment.

10. AI-Powered Sales Insights:Use AI-driven tools to gain insights into prospect behavior and sentiment, helping your sales team make more informed decisions.

Real-World Examples

Let's examine how some notable companies have excelled in modern sales strategies:

1. Salesforce: Salesforce offers a suite of sales and CRM solutions that empower businesses to streamline sales processes, gain valuable insights, and enhance customer engagement.

2. HubSpot: HubSpot provides a range of sales and marketing automation tools, including CRM, email marketing, and lead nurturing. HubSpot's inbound sales and marketing methodology helps businesses attract, engage, and delight customers, leading to higher conversion rates and customer satisfaction.

3. Oracle: Oracle's Sales Cloud offers comprehensive sales automation, analytics, and reporting tools that help businesses optimize their sales processes and enhance customer relationships.

4. IBM: IBM leverages data analytics and AI to provide solutions that enable predictive sales insights, helping businesses make informed decisions and improve sales effectiveness.

5. Slack: Slack combines a user-friendly communication platform with integrations for sales and customer support tools, streamlining internal communications and customer interactions.

These companies demonstrate how modern sales strategies, combined with technology and data-driven insights, can lead to successful customer engagement and conversion.

Closing Thoughts

In the dynamic landscape of 2024, mastering sales strategies is essential for converting leads into loyal customers. This chapter has provided you with a roadmap to navigate the complexities of the modern marketplace, from understanding the sales funnel to implementing data-driven strategies and adapting to the evolving landscape.

Chapter 10

Customer Service Excellence - Building Lasting Relationships Through Exceptional Support in 2024

Welcome to Chapter 10 of "Mastering Business Planning in 2024." In this chapter, we will explore the paramount significance of customer service excellence. In the ever-evolving landscape of modern business, exceptional customer service is the cornerstone of building lasting relationships with your customers, attracting buyers, and fostering loyalty in 2024 and beyond.

The Critical Role of Customer Service

Exceptional customer service is more than just a department within your business; it's the face and heartbeat of your brand. In 2024, the importance of delivering unparalleled customer service has reached new heights. Here's why understanding the role of customer service is paramount:

- Customer Retention:Outstanding customer service is a key driver of customer loyalty and retention. Happy customers are more likely to return and recommend your business to others.

- Competitive Advantage: Exceptional service sets your brand apart in a crowded marketplace, creating a unique selling proposition.

- Brand Image and Reputation:Customer service shapes your brand's image and reputation. Positive experiences lead to favorable reviews and word-of-mouth marketing.

- Problem Resolution: Efficient customer service helps resolve issues and complaints swiftly, mitigating potential damage to your brand's reputation.

- Data and Feedback: Customer service interactions provide invaluable data and feedback that can be leveraged to improve products, services, and customer experiences.

To excel in 2024, businesses must prioritize customer service excellence, treating every customer interaction as an opportunity to delight, retain, and attract buyers.

The Evolution of Customer Service

Customer service has evolved in lockstep with technological advancements and shifting consumer preferences. The traditional model of reactive service has given way to proactive, personalized, and multi-channel support. Understanding this evolution is crucial for crafting effective customer service strategies. Key trends in the evolution of customer service include:

1. Proactive Support: Modern customer service anticipates customer needs and seeks to address issues before they become problems.

2.Personalization:Tailoring customer interactions based on individual preferences and purchase history is a hallmark of contemporary service.

3. Multichannel Support: Providing customer service across various channels – from

traditional phone and email to chat, social media, and mobile apps – is now expected.

4. Self-Service Options: Businesses offer knowledge bases, FAQs, and interactive guides that allow customers to find solutions independently.

5. Automation and AI: Chatbots and virtual assistants use AI to provide real-time support and resolve common issues.

6. Social Media Engagement:Businesses actively engage with customers on social media, responding to questions and concerns in real time.

7. Data-Driven Insights: Customer interactions provide valuable data that can inform business decisions and improve the customer experience.

Crafting a Customer Service Strategy

A customer service strategy is not a one-size-fits-all approach but should be tailored to your business, industry, and customer base. To craft a successful strategy, consider these key components:

1. Customer-Centric Culture: Foster a company culture that places the customer at the center of every decision, encouraging all employees to prioritize the customer experience.

2. Customer Journey Mapping: Understand your customer's journey, identifying key touchpoints where exceptional service can be delivered.

3. Support Team Training: Equip your support team with the skills, knowledge, and tools required to provide excellent service, including effective communication and problem-solving.

4. Multichannel Approach: Provide customer service through multiple channels, ensuring that customers can reach you in their preferred way.

5. Self-Service Options: Offer a comprehensive self-service knowledge base and interactive tools for customers who prefer to solve problems on their own.

6. Automation and AI: Implement automation and AI-driven solutions for efficiency, including chatbots for routine inquiries and data analytics for personalization.

7. Customer Feedback and Surveys: Actively seek customer feedback through surveys, reviews, and direct feedback channels, using this input to make improvements.

8. Data Analytics: Utilize data analytics to gain insights into customer behavior, preferences, and pain points, allowing you to continuously refine your customer service.

9. Continuous Improvement:Develop a culture of continuous improvement, with regular

reviews of customer service processes and customer feedback.

10. Employee Empowerment: Empower your customer service team to take ownership of issues and provide solutions rather than relying on scripts.

Adapting to the 2024 Landscape

In 2024, customer service must adapt to changing consumer expectations and emerging technologies. Consider these strategies to ensure your customer service remains effective:

1. AI and Automation: Leverage AI and automation to enhance the customer service

experience. AI-driven chatbots and virtual assistants can provide instant support.

2. Omnichannel Support:Ensure a seamless customer experience across multiple channels, allowing customers to switch between them without losing context.

3. Personalization: Use data-driven personalization to tailor interactions and support to individual customers.

4. Social Media Engagement: Be present and responsive on social media platforms where your customers are active.

5. Self-Service Advancements: Continuously enhance self-service options with interactive

guides and AI-powered search tools, ensuring they are accessible and user-friendly on mobile devices.

6. Mobile Optimization (Continued): Optimize your customer service for mobile users to provide a smooth and convenient experience on smartphones and tablets.

7. Emotional Intelligence: Train your support team to understand and empathize with customer emotions, offering a more compassionate and human-centered approach to service.

8. Feedback Integration: Act on customer feedback by integrating it into your improvement processes. Share insights from

feedback with your team to foster a culture of continuous learning.

9. 24/7 Availability: Explore options for providing round-the-clock customer support, whether through global teams, automated responses, or outsourcing.

10. Predictive Service:Use data analytics and AI to predict customer needs and issues, offering solutions before customers even realize they need them.

Real-World Examples

Let's examine how some renowned companies have excelled in providing exceptional customer service:

1. Zappos: Zappos is renowned for its commitment to delivering extraordinary customer service. The company empowers its support team to go above and beyond to satisfy customers.

2. Amazon: Amazon's customer service is known for its efficiency and customer-centric approach, including a robust self-service system and hassle-free returns.

3. Apple: Apple combines in-store support with online resources and responsive customer

service teams to provide comprehensive support for its products.

4. Ritz-Carlton: Ritz-Carlton sets the standard for luxury customer service, focusing on personalization, anticipation of customer needs, and exceptional hospitality.

5. Disney: Disney's theme parks and resorts offer legendary customer service, emphasizing the creation of magical and unforgettable experiences for visitors.

These companies exemplify the power of exceptional customer service in building lasting relationships with customers and fostering brand loyalty.

Closing Thoughts

In the dynamic landscape of 2024, exceptional customer service is the linchpin to building lasting relationships with your customers. This chapter has equipped you with the insights and strategies needed to excel in customer service, from understanding the evolving role of support

to crafting effective strategies and adapting to

the modern landscape.

Chapter 11

Leveraging Technology and Innovation - A Pathway to Future Success in Business

Welcome to Chapter 11 of "Mastering Business Planning in 2024." In this chapter, we explore the dynamic intersection of technology and innovation as a pathway to future success in business. In a landscape marked by unprecedented digital transformation, embracing technology and fostering innovation is not just an option but a necessity to attract buyers and remain competitive in 2024 and beyond.

The Technology-Driven Revolution

The world of business is undergoing a profound transformation, largely driven by technological advancements. These innovations are not just altering the way business is conducted; they are fundamentally reshaping industries and consumer behavior. Here's why understanding the technology-driven revolution is essential:

- Market Disruption: Technological innovations have led to market disruptions, challenging traditional business models and creating new opportunities.

- Customer Expectations: Modern consumers expect seamless digital experiences, from online shopping to customer service, making technology a central component of customer satisfaction.

- Efficiency and Productivity: Technology streamlines operations, enhances productivity, and reduces costs, contributing to a competitive edge.

- Data-Driven Insights: Data analytics provide a wealth of insights into customer behavior, market trends, and business performance, enabling data-driven decision-making.

To excel in 2024, businesses must embrace technology and innovation, adopting a proactive stance that integrates these elements into every aspect of their operations.

The Innovation Spectrum

Innovation is not a one-size-fits-all concept; it spans a spectrum from incremental improvements to disruptive breakthroughs. Understanding this spectrum is critical for tailoring innovation strategies to the unique needs and goals of your business. Here's an overview:

1. Incremental Innovation: Small, gradual improvements to existing products, services, or processes. These optimizations yield significant results over time.

2. Product Innovation: Creation of entirely new products or significant improvements to existing ones. Product innovation can open up new markets and revenue streams.

3. Process Innovation: Focuses on improving how things are done within your organization, leading to increased efficiency, cost savings, and resource management.

4. Business Model Innovation: Rethinking fundamental ways your business creates, delivers, and captures value. Business model innovation can lead to entirely new revenue streams or customer segments.

5. Service Innovation: Creation of new or improved services to better meet customer needs, often complementing product innovation and enhancing customer experiences.

6. Disruptive Innovation: The most radical form of innovation, creating new products, services, or technologies that disrupt and transform entire

industries. Disruptive innovation often requires a high degree of risk-taking.

Strategies for Leveraging Technology and Innovation

Fostering a culture of technology and innovation is not just about having the latest gadgets; it's about creating an environment where these ideas can thrive. Here are strategies to cultivate technology and innovation in your business:

1. Leadership Support:** Innovation starts at the top. Leaders must encourage and support technology and innovation initiatives, leading by example.

2. Cross-Functional Collaboration: Encourage employees from different departments to collaborate, bringing diverse perspectives to problem-solving.

3. Idea Generation Platforms: Create platforms for employees to submit, discuss, and refine ideas. These can be through digital tools, brainstorming sessions, or innovation challenges.

4. Data-Driven Insights: Use data to gain insights into customer behavior, market trends, and areas in need of improvement.

5. Customer Feedback: Act on customer feedback and involve customers in the co-creation of products and services.

6. Prototyping: Develop prototypes or minimum viable products to test new ideas and gather feedback before full-scale implementation.

7. Risk Tolerance: Encourage calculated risk-taking. Innovations often involve some degree of uncertainty and risk.

8. Continuous Learning: Invest in employee training and development to keep skills and knowledge up to date.

9. Patience and Persistence: Recognize that not all innovations will succeed immediately. Persistence is key to refining and adapting ideas.

10. Open to Failure: Understand that not all innovation attempts will succeed, and failure is part of the innovation process. Learn from failures and apply those lessons to future efforts.

Embracing Technological Advancements

The rapidly evolving technological landscape presents numerous opportunities for businesses. By embracing technological advancements, you can enhance efficiency, reach new markets, and meet the changing expectations of consumers.

Key strategies for leveraging technology include:

1. Digital Transformation: Embrace digital technologies to enhance your operations, reach, and customer experiences. This includes adopting cloud computing, mobile apps, and digital tools to streamline your processes.

2. Artificial Intelligence (AI): Explore AI applications such as chatbots, virtual assistants, and data analysis to improve customer experiences, streamline operations, and gain insights into customer behavior.

3. Augmented Reality (AR) and Virtual Reality (VR): Consider how AR and VR can enhance

customer engagement and experiences, especially in industries like retail and entertainment.

4. Cybersecurity: Invest in robust cybersecurity measures to protect customer data and build trust in an era of increased cyber threats.

5. Sustainability and ESG Initiatives: Consider sustainability and environmental, social, and governance (ESG) initiatives to align with changing consumer values and regulatory requirements.

6. Internet of Things (IoT): Explore IoT technologies for data collection and automation,

which can improve operations and enhance customer experiences.

7. Automation: Implement process automation to streamline routine tasks, reducing costs and freeing up employees for more strategic work.

8. Machine Learning: Utilize machine learning algorithms to analyze data, predict customer behavior, and make real-time decisions.

9. 5G Technology: Explore the possibilities of 5G technology, which promises faster and more reliable connections, enabling new applications and services.

10. Digital Marketing: Leverage the latest digital marketing techniques, such as personalized

content, retargeting, and marketing automation, to reach your audience effectively.

Real-World Examples

Let's look at some companies that have excelled in leveraging technology and innovation:

1. Tesla: Tesla revolutionized the automotive industry by pioneering electric vehicles, autonomous driving technology, and over-the-air updates.

2. Apple: Apple consistently introduces innovative products such as the iPhone, iPad, and Apple Watch, combined with an ecosystem

that offers seamless integration and customer experience.

3. Amazon: Amazon's use of technology and innovation in its supply chain, delivery systems, and cloud computing services has positioned it as a global e-commerce and technology giant.

4. Netflix: Netflix transformed the entertainment industry by pioneering streaming services and investing in data-driven content recommendations.

5. Google: Google continues to innovate with products and services such as Google Search, Maps, and the Android operating system, making them central to our digital lives.

These companies showcase how embracing technology and fostering innovation can lead to industry disruption and competitive advantages, making them attractive to buyers and loyal customers.

Closing Thoughts

In the ever-evolving landscape of 2024, technology and innovation are the catalysts for future business success. This chapter has provided you with insights and strategies to harness the power of technology and innovation, from understanding the innovation spectrum to crafting strategies that foster innovation and adapt to technological advancements.

Chapter 12

Sustainability and Corporate Social Responsibility - A New Imperative for Business Success in 2024

Welcome to Chapter 12 of "Mastering Business Planning in 2024." In this chapter, we will explore the critical importance of sustainability and corporate social responsibility (CSR) as a new imperative for business success. In a world where environmental and social concerns have come to the forefront, integrating sustainability and CSR into your business strategy is not only ethical but also a strategy to attract buyers and thrive in 2024 and beyond.

The Sustainability Revolution

The world is experiencing a sustainability revolution, driven by a growing awareness of environmental challenges, social inequalities, and the urgent need for responsible business practices. Sustainability is no longer a buzzword but an essential component of a successful business strategy. Here's why understanding the sustainability revolution is crucial:

- Consumer Expectations: Modern consumers are increasingly concerned about the environmental and social impact of their purchases. Businesses that align with these values are more attractive to buyers.

- Regulatory Changes: Governments and international bodies are implementing regulations that require businesses to reduce their environmental footprint and improve social responsibility.

- Cost Savings: Sustainable practices can lead to cost savings through reduced resource consumption and waste, making businesses more competitive.

- Brand Image:Embracing sustainability and CSR can enhance brand image, attracting conscious consumers and fostering loyalty.

To excel in 2024, businesses must prioritize sustainability and CSR, making them integral to their operations and values.

Understanding Sustainability and CSR

Sustainability and CSR encompass a broad spectrum of practices and initiatives, reflecting a commitment to addressing environmental and social challenges. Here's an overview of these concepts:

1. Sustainability: Sustainability involves practices that aim to minimize the environmental impact of a business while ensuring long-term economic viability. Key areas include energy efficiency, waste reduction, responsible sourcing, and carbon footprint reduction.

2. Corporate Social Responsibility (CSR): CSR encompasses a business's efforts to contribute positively to society and address social issues. This may involve philanthropy, community engagement, employee well-being, diversity and inclusion, and ethical business practices.

3. Environmental, Social, and Governance (ESG): ESG refers to a set of criteria that investors use to assess a company's performance in environmental, social, and governance areas. Businesses that meet ESG standards are often seen as more attractive to investors and buyers.

4. Sustainable Development Goals (SDGs):The United Nations has outlined 17 Sustainable Development Goals, addressing global challenges such as poverty, inequality, climate change, and clean water. Many businesses align their sustainability efforts with these goals.

5. Circular Economy: The circular economy aims to minimize waste and maximize the use of

resources by designing products for durability and recycling and reusing materials.

6. Carbon Neutrality: Achieving carbon neutrality involves balancing the greenhouse gas emissions a business produces by investing in carbon offsetting projects.

7. Social Impact: Social impact initiatives focus on creating positive change in communities through philanthropic efforts, employee volunteer programs, and partnerships with non-profit organizations.

Strategies for Sustainability and CSR

Integrating sustainability and CSR into your business requires a well-thought-out strategy. Here are key strategies to adopt:

1. Leadership Commitment: Leaders must champion sustainability and CSR, setting an example for the entire organization.

2. Stakeholder Engagement: Involve employees, customers, suppliers, and the community in sustainability and CSR efforts, building a sense of shared responsibility.

3. Impact Assessment: Assess your current environmental and social impact, identifying areas for improvement.

4. Goal Setting: Set clear, measurable goals for sustainability and CSR efforts, with defined timelines.

5. Supply Chain Responsibility: Ensure your supply chain adheres to sustainable and ethical practices, including responsible sourcing and fair labor practices.

6. Environmental Initiatives: Implement initiatives such as energy efficiency, waste reduction, and water conservation in your operations.

7. Employee Engagement:Engage employees in sustainability and CSR efforts, fostering a sense of purpose and commitment.

8. Reporting and Transparency: Communicate your sustainability and CSR efforts transparently to stakeholders through reports and disclosure mechanisms.

9. Risk Assessment: Identify and mitigate risks associated with environmental and social issues that could impact your business.

10. Continuous Improvement:Continuously assess and refine your sustainability and CSR strategies based on performance and changing circumstances.

Building a Sustainable Brand

Sustainability and CSR can be a powerful tool in building a sustainable brand that attracts conscious buyers. Key strategies include:

1. Brand Alignment: Ensure that sustainability and CSR efforts align with your brand's values and messaging.

2. Storytelling: Tell compelling stories about your sustainability and CSR initiatives to engage customers emotionally.

3. Transparency: Be transparent about your efforts, progress, and challenges in sustainability and CSR.

4. Sustainable Product Development:Design products with sustainability in mind, offering

eco-friendly options and highlighting their environmental benefits.

5. Green Marketing:Use eco-friendly marketing practices and materials to reflect your commitment to sustainability.

6. Customer Engagement:Involve customers in sustainability initiatives, allowing them to participate in positive change.

7. Partnerships: Collaborate with like-minded organizations, non-profits, and environmental groups to amplify the impact of your sustainability efforts.

8. Feedback and Improvement: Actively seek feedback from customers on your sustainability

and CSR efforts and make continuous improvements based on their input.

9. Certified Labels: Consider obtaining relevant sustainability and CSR certifications that can add credibility to your claims.

10. Measurable Impact: Showcase the measurable impact of your sustainability initiatives to demonstrate tangible results.

Sustainability and CSR in Action

Let's explore how some prominent companies have successfully integrated sustainability and CSR into their operations:

1. Patagonia: Patagonia, an outdoor apparel company, is renowned for its environmental commitment. The company uses recycled materials, donates a percentage of profits to environmental causes, and encourages customers to repair rather than replace their products.

2. Unilever: Unilever, a consumer goods giant, has made sustainability a central part of its business model. The company has set ambitious goals to reduce its environmental impact, improve social impact, and promote responsible sourcing.

3. IKEA: IKEA, the global furniture retailer, is committed to sustainability and responsible

sourcing. They have set ambitious goals to become climate positive, circular, and fair to all.

4. Danone: Danone, a multinational food products corporation, places a strong emphasis on CSR by focusing on sustainable agriculture, responsible packaging, and social responsibility.

5. Microsoft: Microsoft is committed to environmental sustainability through efforts to become carbon negative and water positive. They are also actively working to expand digital access to underserved communities.

These companies demonstrate that sustainability and CSR can be integral to their business models, not only attracting conscious buyers but also contributing to their long-term success.

Closing Thoughts

In the dynamic landscape of 2024, sustainability and corporate social responsibility are no longer optional; they are integral to business success. This chapter has provided you with insights and strategies to integrate sustainability and CSR into your business, from understanding the sustainability revolution to crafting strategies that build a sustainable brand and make a positive impact.

Chapter 13

Adaptability and Resilience - Navigating Uncertainty for Business Success in 2024

Welcome to Chapter 13 of "Mastering Business Planning in 2024." In this chapter, we will delve into the critical importance of adaptability and resilience in the face of uncertainty. The modern business landscape is characterized by rapid changes and unforeseen challenges. To attract buyers and succeed in 2024 and beyond, businesses must prioritize adaptability and resilience as core attributes of their strategy.

The New Normal: Uncertainty

The world is in a state of perpetual change and uncertainty. Global events, technological advancements, and shifting consumer behaviors have made uncertainty a constant companion in business. Here's why understanding the new normal of uncertainty is crucial:

- Accelerated Change: The pace of change in technology, markets, and consumer preferences has accelerated, requiring businesses to adapt quickly.

-Global Events:Events such as pandemics, economic crises, and geopolitical shifts can disrupt industries and markets unexpectedly.

- Consumer Empowerment: Consumers are more informed, vocal, and demanding, which necessitates businesses to be agile and responsive to their needs.

-Technological Disruption: Emerging technologies can reshape industries and create both opportunities and challenges for businesses. To excel in 2024, businesses must embrace uncertainty as a given and develop the capabilities to navigate it effectively.

Understanding Adaptability and Resilience

Adaptability and resilience are not just buzzwords but essential attributes for business success in an uncertain world. Here's an overview of these concepts:

1. Adaptability: Adaptability involves the ability to change and adjust in response to evolving circumstances. It means being flexible, open to new ideas, and willing to experiment to find the best path forward.

2. Resilience: Resilience is the capacity to withstand and recover from adversity. Resilient businesses are those that can endure shocks,

such as economic downturns or disruptions, and continue to thrive.

3. Business Continuity:Business continuity planning involves preparing for unexpected disruptions and having strategies in place to maintain critical operations in times of crisis.

4. Agile Business Models: Agile business models are designed to respond quickly to changes, making it easier to pivot when necessary and take advantage of new opportunities.

5. Scenario Planning: Scenario planning involves envisioning multiple potential future scenarios and preparing strategies for each,

allowing businesses to be prepared for a range of outcomes.

6. Risk Management: Effective risk management involves identifying and mitigating potential risks that could impact the business.

7.Employee Training and Development: Training employees in adaptability, problem-solving, and resilience can help the entire organization navigate uncertain times effectively.

8. Technology Adoption: Embracing technology can enhance adaptability, helping businesses to stay competitive and pivot rapidly when needed.

9. Customer Engagement: Engaging with customers, gathering their feedback, and adapting to their changing needs is crucial for long-term success.

10. Cultural Transformation: Creating a culture that values adaptability and resilience is essential. This begins with leadership and permeates throughout the organization.

Strategies for Adaptability and Resilience

Building adaptability and resilience into your business strategy requires thoughtful planning and proactive steps. Here are key strategies to consider:

1. Diversify Revenue Streams: Avoid relying heavily on a single revenue source. Diversification can provide a safety net in uncertain times.

2. Financial Reserves:Maintain financial reserves that can sustain the business during downturns or disruptions.

3. Market Research:Continuously monitor market trends, consumer behaviors, and emerging technologies to anticipate changes.

4. Scenario Planning:Develop and regularly update scenarios that envision potential future challenges and opportunities.

5. Cross-Training:Cross-train employees so that they can take on different roles when needed, improving workforce flexibility.

6. Collaboration: Build partnerships and collaborations with other businesses that can provide support and resources in times of need.

7. Supply Chain Resilience: Ensure your supply chain is robust and adaptable to handle disruptions.

8. Digital Transformation:Embrace digital technologies and automation to improve

efficiency, reach customers, and adapt to changing circumstances.

9. Data-Driven Decision-Making: Use data analytics to inform decisions, identify trends, and adapt strategies based on insights.

10. Customer Feedback: Actively seek customer feedback to understand their needs and adapt your products and services accordingly.

Fostering a Culture of Adaptability and Resilience

Creating a culture of adaptability and resilience is essential for organizational success. Key strategies to foster this culture include:

1. Leadership Example: Leaders should model adaptability and resilience in their decision-making and responses to challenges.

2.Communication:Open and transparent communication helps employees understand the reasons behind changes and disruptions, fostering a sense of shared purpose.

3. Learning and Development: Invest in employee training and development to improve their skills, especially in areas related to adaptability and resilience.

4. Employee Well-Being:Prioritize employee well-being to ensure they are physically and

mentally healthy, as this contributes to their ability to adapt and remain resilient.

5. Rewards and Recognition: Acknowledge and reward employees who demonstrate adaptability and resilience, reinforcing their importance within the organization.

6. Cross-Functional Teams: Create cross-functional teams that bring together individuals with diverse skills and experiences to tackle challenges from different angles.

7. Agile Processes: Implement agile processes that allow for rapid adjustments and pivots in response to changing circumstances.

8. Diversity and Inclusion: A diverse and inclusive workplace brings different perspectives and approaches to problem-solving, enhancing adaptability.

9. Innovation Initiatives: Encourage employees to propose and experiment with innovative ideas that can lead to adaptability and resilience.

10. Adaptability Training:Offer training in adaptability and resilience to employees at all levels of the organization.

Adapting to the 2024 Landscape

In 2024, businesses must adapt to a landscape characterized by continued technological advancements, shifting consumer behaviors, and global uncertainties. Key strategies for adapting to this landscape include:

1. Digital Transformation: Embrace digital technologies, including artificial intelligence, big data analytics, and automation, to stay competitive and meet changing consumer expectations.

2. Remote Work and Flexible Work Models : Ensure your business can operate effectively with remote and flexible work arrangements, accommodating changing work preferences and global events.

3. Resilient Supply Chains:Strengthen your supply chain resilience by diversifying sources, using data to predict disruptions, and implementing technology-driven solutions for greater visibility and control.

4. Crisis Management:Develop and regularly update crisis management plans that address various scenarios, ensuring your business can respond swiftly and effectively to unforeseen challenges.

5. Customer-Centric Approach: Maintain a customer-centric approach by using data and feedback to adapt to changing customer preferences and expectations.

6. Environmental Responsibility:Embrace environmental sustainability as an integral part of your business, meeting the demands of eco-conscious consumers and regulators.

7. Talent Acquisition and Retention:Attract and retain adaptable and resilient talent who can thrive in uncertain environments and contribute to your business's success.

8. Market Monitoring:Continuously monitor market trends, competitive landscapes, and emerging technologies to adapt your strategies proactively.

9. Partnerships and Collaborations:Explore partnerships and collaborations with other

businesses and organizations that can enhance your adaptability and resilience.

10. Innovative Product Development:Focus on innovative product and service development to meet changing customer needs and to stay ahead of the competition.

Real-World Examples

Let's explore how some well-known companies have successfully navigated uncertainty through adaptability and resilience:

1. Amazon: Amazon's ability to pivot from an online bookstore to a global e-commerce and

technology giant showcases its adaptability and resilience.

2. Zoom: Zoom quickly adapted to the increased demand for remote communication during the COVID-19 pandemic, demonstrating agility in responding to unforeseen challenges.

3. Ford: Ford has embraced technological advancements and shifts in consumer preferences by investing in electric vehicles and autonomous driving technology while maintaining its legacy in the automotive industry.

4. IBM: IBM's transformation from a hardware-focused company to a leader in cloud

computing and artificial intelligence illustrates its adaptability in staying relevant in a rapidly changing tech landscape.

5. Procter & Gamble: Procter & Gamble, a consumer goods powerhouse, has consistently adapted to changing consumer needs and preferences, remaining a leader in its industry for decades.

These companies demonstrate how adaptability and resilience are crucial for not only surviving but thriving in the face of uncertainty, making them attractive to buyers and investors.

Closing Thoughts

In the dynamic landscape of 2024, adaptability and resilience are not just survival skills; they are vital attributes for thriving in the face of uncertainty. This chapter has provided you with insights and strategies to make adaptability and resilience integral to your business strategy, from understanding the new normal of uncertainty to crafting a culture of adaptability and resilience and adapting to the 2024 landscape.

Conclusion

As we reach the conclusion of "Mastering Business Planning in 2024," we've embarked on a journey through the ever-evolving landscape of modern business. In these pages, we've explored a multitude of strategies and insights, each a stepping stone towards your success in the dynamic year of 2024.

In this transformative era, businesses must be equipped not just to survive but to thrive in a landscape defined by change, uncertainty, and the relentless march of innovation. The path to success is paved with agility, adaptability, and resilience. Here, we've highlighted the vital role of adaptability and resilience, proving that these attributes are not mere survival skills but potent weapons for those who dare to excel.

But beyond adaptability and resilience, we've laid a comprehensive foundation for building your success story. From crafting a compelling business plan to understanding the nuances of financial management, marketing mastery, and the art of exceptional customer service, you have been armed with a comprehensive toolkit to meet the challenges of 2024 head-on.

We've navigated through the complexities of sustainability and corporate social responsibility, demonstrating that business success is intrinsically linked to ethical practices, environmental responsibility, and a commitment to making a positive impact on society.

We've shown you how to harness the power of technology and innovation, revealing that staying ahead in the business world means embracing emerging technologies, fostering a culture of innovation, and leading the charge in an era of perpetual disruption.

Throughout this journey, we've woven together real-world examples, best practices, and actionable strategies to empower you. Our goal has been to equip you with the knowledge, tools, and insights you need to make your mark in the world of business in 2024.

As you embark on your business endeavors, remember that every challenge is an opportunity, every change a chance to adapt and grow, and every interaction a step toward building lasting relationships. In the fast-paced world of 2024, your success hinges on your ability to master these principles, seize every opportunity, and rise to the occasion.

We hope this book has ignited your entrepreneurial spirit, inspired you to take action, and armed you with the knowledge and skills to succeed. In 2024, the world of business is waiting for your unique vision, your innovation, and your resilience.

Now, go forth and make your mark. The world is yours to conquer, and the future is yours to shape. Here's to your success in the exciting year of 2024 and beyond.

www.ingramcontent.com/pod-product-compliance
Lightning Source LLC
Chambersburg PA
CBHW072150290526
45794CB00004B/1472